# Art of Enlightenment

# Art of Enlightenment

Poems by

Wayne-Daniel Berard

Cover design by Shay Culligan
Cover artwork by Scott McCallister

ISBN: 978-1-954353-65-7

Kelsay Books
502 South 1040 East, A-119
American Fork, Utah, 84003

*To my late parents,*
*Genevieve Berard, 9/18/18, lymphoma,*
*Albert J. Berard, 4/27/20, Covid 19.*

*For my Christine, in all things.*

# Acknowledgments

Many thanks to the publications in which versions of the following poems have appeared:

*Amethyst Review:* "age of physics," "Daniel," "Good Friday at the Gardner," "Tahira," "Peter"
*Bagels with the Bards:* "Book," " bottles"
*Clementine Unbound:* "Certain Facility"
*The Daily Drunk:* "Sonnet 73 in Allergy Season"
*Maximum Tilt:* "For," "Not Just Another Poem About Mary Oliver"
*North of Oxford Review:* "Christine in my Crisis," "Passover in Plague Time," "My Father's Covid"
*Panoplyzine:* "lord and taylor"
*Pensive:* "my dear depression," "A Jew at the BLM Rally"
*Red Eft:* "Clippers"
*Rockvale Review:* "passing"


With deepest thanks to Deborah Leipziger, *Soul-Lit,* Carolyn Martin, Delisa Hargrove, Karen Kelsay, Emily Rebekah Green, and to Scott McCallister for his amazing cover photo.

# Contents

His utmost being…

His utmost being simply is to give.
Wholly to die, or wholly, else, to live!
—*Stephen Spender*

# art of enlightenment

We walked to the
pond and the island
the day dad died
I said "I think I've
found the meaning
of life—Art. Merton
says it enables us
to find ourselves
and lose ourselves
at the same time. I'm
writing my best poetry
right now." You motioned
toward the pizza box the
chipotle bag the bud cans
scattered beyond the over
flowing bin. "You get
those over there," you
said. "I'll start here."

Wholly to die...

# Clippers

I may not be able
to keep my mother
from fading like
an old photograph
before my eyes
as lymphoma
undevelops her
nor can I convince
the fragmenting
selves who are
my father that
the mute woman
beside him in the
common room is
not plotting against
him but I can
refuse to not notice
the frigging nerve
of that vine shooting
itself impossibly
from the chain link
into the personal space
of this poor maple
wrapping itself
insidiously around
and around and around it
I can take these bloody big
shears and clip the living
hell out of the goddamn
thing and feel
the tree breathe that much easier
and myself coming back
tomorrow.

# Flight

Older and
heavier most
of us anyway
Mom seems
lighter and
if not younger
rechilded
she crumps
in her covers
like a 7:00 bedtime
and if not for
the blankets I
swear she would
float away most
of us become more
convinced of gravity
less faith in free
flight Mom defies
all pulls, including
mine and wingless
seems ready to
rise

# My Mother and King David

At some point you say to yourself
"I can live with this forever"
if mom never gets better
never gets worse
you remove yourself
from the equation
without being able to
solve it yes you can go
to the nursing home every
day of your life yes you
can just watch her
not watching you
can answer
the unanswerable
by no longer asking.
the Process of Godding
crawls in mysterious ways
"How long?" The Psalmist
often asks but I don't
not anymore now I
center on the meaning
of that long dead
still alive singer's
name: *Beloved.*

# Praying for my mother

When I was 6–7,
I prayed she would hide me
(should my birth mother
sudden our door)
When I was 10–12,
I prayed she would
protect me from
the bullying universe
(she tried, worsening)
When I was 15–16
I prayed she would
disappear, when I was
22–23 I prayed she would
mind her own damn business,
When I was 32–35
I prayed she would watch
the kids every now and then
(exhaustion heavier than
baggage), when I was 45–50
I prayed she'd understand
the divorce (she didn't but
stayed put) at 66
I pray for
swiftness of passage
without suddenness with
bullyless nurses who make
it their soft business to help
her disappear (but not
before my children show up)
I pray that she will stay
not one more moment from
her great, remothering birth.

# The god Shiva, Baking

There was no
banana bread like
my mother's banana
bread hers as well the
archetype of tomato
soup cake forget Plato
the Genevievic Forms
of strawberry rhubarb
or apple pie were definitional
what was her secret?
looking back
I see her mashing over-
ripe yellowness with a
giddy zeal laughing to
herself at the secret of
battered soup pummeling
thawed strawberries into
smithereens with such vengeance
(she never bought them pulverized)
then
eagerly she'd puncture
each creation while in oven
like Lord Shiva with his trishul
if nothing stuck
she was done.

# o earth

my mother is
not hanging on
she has no
dear life she
is waiting for
no one always
have I loved
the stubbornness
of life on this planet
persisting through
plastic strangulation
climatic riot children's
indifference but now
the two-edged
sword of indefatigability
needs to be unbeaten
caressed released into
ploughshare
        welcome
        her o earth

# The Shaman's Dumpster

When I die,
do not toss my
last box of stuff
into the dumpster
(as I just did with
my mom's) rather,
repersonalize the contents
toss the photos keep
the frames empty the
wallets (ID's memberships
funeral cards) tear out all
but blank pages in the
address book detrash
them put them in a little
pile out back or better
by the walking path
that cuts cross town
like a journey a shrine
like the room at the end
of a baby shower
I'll come by whoever
I might be and pick it all
up like take out on a Saturday
night a soul hungry for form
for detail why didn't I do
that with my mom's box
you ask?
her catholic words could never
talk about my gifts only on
that last night her hungered-out
fear-formed eyes
pleaded with mine "please
please don't let
me come back here"

25

# passing

the passing of my mother
is just that    my mother
passes in a black '48 Plymouth
a bowler hat on wheels  she
is driving  she never drove
never learned dad drove her
then me  my mother
passes smiling not stopping

# age of physics

the quantum bits
zap in and out
*where? where? where?*
my father comes and goes
and comes is it some
other chair in some
other nursing home that
holds the man I knew
when he disappears from
*here* and reappears is
the food better *there*?
can he still play cribbage
and laugh and recognize
some alternative son in
that place to which he
flickers right before my
eyes? Is he a wave there
still afroth with possibilities
so different from the particles
of himself that seem to drop
like pieces of personhood dried
and falling like last year's snow?

# Valentine's Day

It had to be today
the day you no
longer knew who
I was
      surrounded
by tackiest dollar
store hearts and
'40s recordings of
apple trees and all
or nothing at all
your blank stare
my pleadings your
head falling to your
own chest mine simply
falling involuntary
abandonments hurt
nonetheless no
one ever means it
*it's not you it's me*
like that type of
lover I'll keep coming
back dad year 97, 98
maybe Valentines
is the right day after
after after all

# Certain Facility

Dad shakes his head
in the nursing home
he never did before
showing only dead certainty
on everything his own
position my brother's and
my worthlessness the
unshakable nature of his
every decision he was sure
and what were we? Now
it's side to side eyes lowered
he doesn't know
                  but that's
not the worst he doesn't
know if he ever knew anything
unwittingly
he prepared the post-modern for
us to find our worth in freest
insecurity now
            Dad is diapered
in notsureness which
he'll allow no diverse
foreignness to change.

# White Dress

He doesn't understand.

Like vision diminishing,
20/20, 20/40, 20/70,
but there are no glasses
for dad's dementia.

"I want you to buy
your mother a white dress
for me," he asks. I blink
back my usual response
that mom died in September.

We are sitting at one square table
of the chess board of Serenity Hill
common room; no one moves, game
interrupted never ended, except
dad's queen's been taken without,
lately, his knowledge.

I answer, "Sure, Dad. Why
a white dress?"
"A wedding dress,"
dad says, "or for bereavement."

I take my trifocals from my face.
"Consider it done."
He understands
more than I
know.

# My Father's Covid

the landing craft
of my father's life
has once again ground
itself on omaha beach
but the iron door
is not dropping
normandy is all gusts
and bluster like always
like him night is falling
and he wonders why
no order to disembark
and why he is alone
in the hold's center
a single candle
gutters and gasps
drowning in the liquid
of its own meltedness
my father wonders if
he's dreaming or gone
crazy until he hears a
woman's voice calling
his name from the darkening
cliffs he recognizes her but
doesn't the candle sputters
he huddles in the corner of
his craft I hope he knows
not to wait for me (denied
permission to board by
executive order) I hope
when the wick exhales
and all the iron falls away
he'll see only enemyless

beach moonlit and know
his one love's call unhiding
in the high hedgerows

# In Memoriam, and Out

Here's a thought
about life:
what if you're every
bit as glad to be
finished with mine?
How early you must
have known the mistake
of your parenting
the herculeaness of
just being dad but
what could you do?
the catholicism of
your veteran's stasis
universality of never
retreating meant
perpetual casualty
you were a prisoner
of conscience yours
wouldn't let you leave
and we became enemy

today on the bike path
that cardinal trailed me
like a taunting escapee
singing no antheming
*just as freefreefreefree*
*freefreefree as you from*
*me*

# In Memory of

*after Auden*

Earth, receive an honored guest,
Al Berard is laid to rest.
True, he could not interpret sighs
or understand my poetry.

But in the nightmare face of war
he looked straight on and swore.
And once returned, he dug
his heels in hard and snug

within the world he knew.
And when he learned a Jew
was his adopted son
he didn't care a bit, just went on

being as he'd always been.
If there is sin in
changelessness, then each
and every poem that can reach

a changeless page is sinful.
My father was a pin but full
of angels dancing in release,
and there are rests in music, peace.

In the handmade clock of life
may its chiming be his wife,
gone before him full two years.
May these verses do for tears.

# Adopted son, birth son

Why do I feel
obliged when you
don't? They never
distinguished us
in any sense of the
word equally dismembered,
unbiased in their degradation
yet here I am
shaving dad because
the nursing home staff
'will get to it,' careful
not to draw what you
alone are: his blood. The
distance is on purpose;
you told me so, unrepentedly.
You know this family, knew
who wouldn't do what, knew
who couldn't help himself from
being and not being
here. I never adopted
any of it nor they any
of me.
It's not the 'will,' not
the 'getting to,' but
the 'it.' Nursing homes
know it. You know it.
My burning, frozen heart
shaves it close.

# Fault

The failed experiment
of my adoption is
almost done only
Dad is left everybody
did their best and
birth family can be
as prone to proactive
amnesia as anyone else
no one really knowing
anyone
        still I thank them
for the lesser form of orphanage
   they wished for progeny
some continuation of themselves
I wanted a home we got
each other and the ever
autumnal comfort of having
held on till the end I
visit the nursing home
twice a week neither of
us nursed or home
December will be nobody's
fault

# my dear depression

don't they understand
they are so much
darker than you and I
my dear depression that
everything is so much
sadder out there than we
are in here compared to
their everyday every post
every newscast you and I
are ecstasy personified it's
a healthy alternative our
melancholy to the pathology
most are married to cheat on
return to it's holy, even, my
dodi li, my beloved downcast
we are our own shabbat
everything stops and we alone
have escaped to keep it  what
do they know the society of shooters
the electors of mad kings
to call us names come
lock the doors my preferable
eclipse don't let their
darkestness in.

# Finding Out You're Jewish 2

The child raised by orcs said
"That's enough. I'm leaving."
"Why don't you write a poem
about it on the way out?" Their
teeth showed when they laughed
and when they didn't. He ran
to men who said "Good, take
this" and handed him a spear.
*I don't want to fulfill my parents'*
*prophecy* he poeticized without
knowing it. "Get out" they stuck
out their tongues. He ran to a
sea and buried himself up to
the voice *I, may I rest in peace—I,*
*who am still living, say, I want*
*the rest of my peace now.* Some
one tall in a tongue he barely
understood without the bite marks
chanted "You're an elf, a High Elf"
the sea parted and he walked
through but left it open
behind him

Note: Italics, *In My Life, On My Life*, Yehuda Amichai

Or wholly, else, to live…

# Asylum

We have all sought
asylum we have all
massed at the border
seeking the America
we'd heard of we have
all been separated from
her we all live in cages
we are none of us counted
so that when asylum seeks us
we'll be nowhere to be found
leaving no choice but
this always this

# A Jew at the BLM rally

I don't know
cannot know
would never presume
to know I refuse to
reverse-freudenschade
your suffering
This much
I can bring here
that work does not
make freedom that
once a slave always
a slave in the sight
of the taskmaster
And speaking
of tasks

# Passover in Plague Time

So this is how it felt
to have it all turn
against you to be
blamed in the burning
choking recesses of
each breath for decisions
by untouchable powers to
watch the river of your
everyday turn red your days
turn nights your very sky
fill with swarms of deadly
devouring tininesses your
massive milieu could not
fend off was this how it felt
when no safe distance
could save first born elders
and silly unschooled children
who gathered regardless
what was the hieroglyph for
"death count?" a human with
no animal head as every beast
had quit us in joyous liberation?
did the symbol rise and widen
grow and dominate until
everything infected everything
with enslavement to remoteness and
collapse? if we were all there back at
sinai then we were all there in giza
and luxor did we say "no, nameless one,
not this! egypt loves its children too
their grandparents are not pharaoh let
our liberation not be bought with plague?"

# The Brazen Age

The time loop
swings backwards in autumn
the green of renewable
leafing reverts to the
September red of iron
then to October bronze
soon we resee the fall
of the Brazen Age
all becomes stone and ice
we huddle in nouveau
caves the rest of the
living world grateful
for our absence
for temporary asylum
from us

# bottles

you lined them up
in the window sill
my little one my
first and talked
with them ornate
bottles two inches
tall swirled red and
golden orange and
violet undulations,
old perfumes you'd
share your secrets
smile and befriend
as you wanted to be
my sad one my daughter
I'd listen from the door
before the Parting did
you keep them? I did.
Added one each year
your birthday until
every window in my
room my house my
life is lined with bottles
when you blow your candles
out this is where the light goes
and for several shining seconds
you are back undivorced and
differently sad I'll wait among
the bottles loving little light

# Saba on the Shore

The grandson I no longer see
("I love Saba more than anybody! I love Saba more than daddy!")
always found his way to my books
and always Haruki Murakami
couldn't yet read
but would stack his novels
one upon another

may this be
no accident

as he goes on to chase
his wild sheep as he dances
dances dances and winds up
that bird that may
or may not
find me on this kafkaesque
shore.

# Daniel

I don't use "step"
as in "step forward"
or worse "step back."
You are my bonus son
the prize I never quite
expected. Too old
for bedtime stories when
I married your mom let
me tell one now: once
upon a theatre in the
middle of things they
held onto your ticket
torn in half
movies had stages then
and when the curtain fell
with credits fading in its
ripples a man would come
and announce the lucky
winner the bonus you
are he and all the lights
come up

# Peter

Keep him safe oh
You Who Save, my
son up on the barricades
who took my '60s stories
home and stands against
the gloriers in the standard
hate the usualness the greed
he could read before he walked
and now he marches balking
not an inch at 6 feet tall a
target unrepentant and I worry.
Should I have spent those childhood
walks imparting Shakespeare
or Godot not Abbie Hoffman and
Rousseau he stands above me in
so much more than height
he's riding on a bus tonight to meet
equality's enemies at some counter-
demonstration, for safety asked me not
to come. Stand by him exonerate
me too who adores him more than
nation cause or You.

# The Reincarnationist Embraces the Digital Library

I remember it
like it was yesterlife.
I preferred the rounded
corner by the fenestrial,
always cool regardless
of the simoom, its breeze
would whisper the dust
from my tablet as
I wrote my heart
in Alexandrines to you,
Aviel, son of the Jewish Quarter,
"our soul needs no conversion, now or evermore."
The stylus pressed
the letters into my
soul like clay. The Great
Library, the perfect locus
for Love Across the
Barriers. How could hate
out-climb these mountains
of scrolls, avalanching
differences? How could
Stephanos Diakanos be
kept from his *ahamet emet?*

They burnt the towers
and us.

Two-thousand-fifty-two
pages, years, later, who knew
Hellenic College consortiumed
with Brandeis? Meet me

at the BPL, beneath the
Sargent murals. *Triumph
of Religion,* indeed. Tell
them we're researching
rediscovered Alexandrines,
their elongated iambs,
η αγάπη νικά, ‏אהבה מנצחת‎,
"love wins, love wins, love wins, love wins, love wins, love wins."

Notes: Alexandrine—a line of verse consisting of six iambs.
      *Ahamet emet*—Hebrew, "Great Love."

# The Doctrine of Signatures

They medievally believed
that God had signed
each medicinal plant
to tell what it would cure
Red for the blood
Yellow for jaundice
My eyes are brown ("full
of crap up to *there"* my
father would rejoke) my
hair beard soul are
white, despite. Combined,
that is the signature of
your warmed-biscotti skin,
curative for whatever ails,
could ever ail, me. Press
its scents against me let me
take my medicine fill me
beyond *there,*
                        undoctrinaire,
miraculous,
                        delicious.

# Sonnet 73 in Allergy Season

That time of year thou mayst see in my nose,
when golden rods or weeds of rags or yew
buds spew their spawn, and ev'ry nostril blows
itself red raw, where once sweet inhales flew.
In me thou see'st the time-out of such scents
As new mown grass or cook outs on the grill.
My sinuses turned into wet cement.
My friends, concerned, inquire if I am ill?
"No," I say, "Just allergies." That "just"
Is nature's cruel understatement, flu's
Other self has sealed up all in crust.
Exhausted is the best that I can do.
    This thou know'st which makes thy love more kind,
    It's midnight, and I'm out of Flonase. Mind?

# TIKKUN, *tikkun*

Hebrew has no
upper case or
lower case here's
why: EVERYTHING
IS IMPORTANT EVER
HEAR US TALKING
CHARGING AND
DISSECTING
FLINGING THE PARTS
AT EACH OTHER
FORGIVING
   and everything is
   the minutest minute
the ordination of
the ordinary nano-
yah in passing moment
   which is why I never
don't pass a student paper
never write a GREAT BIG
F but in my whispering
cursive sign only "see me?"
"And who knows but that you
have come," Mordecai tells Esther,
"to this great kingdom for such a time
as this and for this very occasion?"


TIKKUN OLAM HEAL THE WORLD


*tikkun talmid heal the student*

# lord and taylor

The intrafaith Jesus
said behold the lilies
of the field uniquely
many inviting curious
bees the interfaith Jesus
said by your fruits will
we know you not the
nuts not the whomp of
your willow the panfaith
Jesus said ye are
gods (though we
said no thank you)
the bad day Jesus
said no one comes
to the father except
through ME the Great
Mother said you need
to calm down so did
T Swift.

# L'internet de dieu

I hope you don't remember me

Thirty years ago
we were on silent retreat
at Mont St. Michelle
You'd trudged? slogged?
(iTranslate for *sloggé,* my
English is not good) the
low-tide shoals between
us and them to buy
*viande de légumes—*
veggies meat?—as
all they served was flesh
I sat reading Elijah and
the still small voice in the
common room with its
fired plaque *Tuez de
Conversation* you approached
and whispered "My stuff
in the fridge is for everyone."
I glared at you as if you
had spit in God's face and
mine
Now I abstain
I saw enough *tuant* in Les Commandos
Hubert I write from Plum Village the
dharma room a hung scroll says
*Practice Stopping* but I just started
searching you I am grateful for
your oddly hyphenated *prénom* I
mean beautifully so instantly I
found you many many shoals

have been my slogging *pardonne-
moi, je supplierai* oh still
                    unforgettable voice.

# Jews in Love

We don't do
"God is love"
not entirely
and that anniversary
tattooed on your arm
um...
we still giggle holding hands
as Lennon's ashes sing
"all you need is" knowing
better
we love like water
like air and yes
like fire elementally
not to be saved
not to be not
alone
just love
just us
like always.

# Good Friday at the Gardner

I'm not ignoring you.
Nor am I minimizing
your suffering—there's
not a minimalist in this
gallery. Rather, it's filled
with images of you half-
smiling, far-sighted,
an enigma unwrapping
its riddle in this garden
of art. The only pain here
is the painfully beautiful.
Is that why I've come?
I no longer believe
in the beauty of pain
—yours or mine—
but I can love the
emerging aprilness
of this day, yet a
winterscape, signed
in its nearest corner
"J of N."

# Dot

Adequacy is
beneath you
(which is why
you can't reach
it) *abundant*
is who you are
*too much* say
the people who
dig a swimming pool
on their beachfront
(with a hand spade
in the 95 degrees and
hate you for not
helping) you are the
ocean they will not
turn to see *copious*
*shoreless.* enoughness
is someone you broke
up with in seventh grade
that's the reason you
can't feel it your beautiful
big eyes don't pick up
smudges of selves
you're the i
not the dot

# If the Buddha Divorced

You are the ex
every man dreams of
non-attached to
narrative; the only
story, levels of love
in your unapartmented
heart it's all one and
you could no more
kick him off your
health insurance
than you could give
yourself the plague
you don't forgive
you fore-give as
if you'd seen your
every incarnation and
knew it would non-end
this way you're the only
person who is
who their dog thinks they are
she shimmies in joy at both
of you and your
unmediated heart here
is my ex's number would
you ring her up like
a zen bell?

# Tahira

Allah said
"If we allow her
this pain, she will
only make poetry
out of it" and one
angel after another
answered "So?"
"Now do you see
why I created them?"
spoke the Beneficent,
the Merciful.

# Uneclipsed

The end of the term
is the end of the moon
its beauty is all its own
as it sails toward its curve
becoming a streak of glow
thinnest sliver of alchemist's
stone heated in the cast iron
blackness some teachers
see this waning (of attention
of energy) as failure I know
that the term like the moon
is going inside inside inside
until poof it's no longer needed
the student like the sky has
become homeoluminecent
I close my eyes like books
awaiting new moons next
terms

# Morning moon

Someone pressed
a silk-white tab
upon the sky
so it wouldn't forget
itself so that
in the heat of the day
the insistence of anger
and the inhuman trafficking
of 5 o'clock
one could refind
one's place
a softest imprint
upon miles
of morning.

# Maybe

It's maybe day
shall I walk to the library
and let the rows of dream
break over me like warm
surf? maybe. shall I
win at scrabble with
the world's most beautiful
woman until her final turn
where she will once again
blessedly destroy my
constructions, my
Helen of Goy? maybe I
could hold in both hands
the warm energy of emerging
interview with a poet who
sings *beauty and compassion*
*fall from the heavens like rain*
maybe I will or I could sit here
in Uncle Abbie's chair and
watch unhurried sun cast
diagonal lines upon the folding
doors of my bedroom closet
(eat your heart out, *sulaam yaakov*)
maybe sleep maybe dream before
after and during this maybe day
definitely indefinite infinitely
un24houred and
                    hastenless.


Note: Hebrew, "Jacob's ladder."

# Not Just Another Poem About Mary Oliver

Yeah, yeah heron, finches, geese.
    when I taught the sonnet it
was her *Last Days* I turned to,
and not so much the snapping
or whistling or booming I wanted
them to hear rhyme undo itself
but retain its shape like an untied
boot after long knotting to feel
meter breathing in fits and starts
but still iambic as her day was long.
All the owls and peonies and whelks
(whatever they are) could not tempt
her from this craft of verse its
only equal taking the air in Coole
Park, inviting her now to share the
wild swans.

# Book

I would no more be
without a book
than I would drive
without my belt,
than I would skip
my meditation or
my dunkin' blueberry
muffin and decaf
extra light with cream
one equal—the coffee
not the book—I would no
more be without a book
than not call you a time
or two a day, beautiful
you, and for the same
reason if given a choice
of last act: book or
prayer, I would unroll
over, say, "What's the
difference?" and read
myself awake.

# For

Our first night together
you cupped my balls in
your hands and I slept
as never before whatever
past whatever future squirreled
in those swirling planetoids laid
themselves to rest there is no
present tense in masculine gender
at least not until then you did not
"have me by them"
never did I feel
less threatened more secure in
your hands I awoke as never
before and ever since
so take
that churches parents kids on
the street corner so this is what

these things are for.

# Beatific Vision

I never understood it
until now sitting across
from you at Bertucci's
your margarita rocks
no salt and your prosciutto
and fig pizza but with shrimp
instead of prosciutto and
that smile defining food drink
light by participation in
your youness I am not
content to see I touch
your hand across the table
Never will I unmeet
you there
O grace abounding
and allowing me to
share

# all along

I wake up with
a start every
morning surprised
to be here then I
turn and see you
my great and only-
needed love my
every instant
you've managed it
again I'd no idea
today was my
surprise party
the dark merely
part of love's
plan all along

His utmost being…

# Christine in my Crisis

We're sitting in the sunroom
the phone is constant
it rings it beeps so
much support "how
is your dad?" "there
for you" I get up from
beside you I don't want
to interrupt your shows
from the kitchen I gaze
every minute of every call
back toward you your
profile defines both sun
and room being light
just by being and being
the one and every place
in which I dwell I'm glad
for all the others I breathe
because of you my constant
occasion the o in each hello

# About the Author

Wayne-Daniel Berard, PhD, is an educator, poet, writer, shaman, and sage. An adoptee and former Franciscan seminarian, his adoption search led him to find and embrace his Jewishness. Wayne-Daniel is an interfaith clergy person, called a Peace Chaplain, as well as a past-life regression leader and energy worker. He publishes broadly in poetry, fiction, and non-fiction. His poetry chapbook, *The Man Who Remembered Heaven,* received the New Eden Award in 2003. His non-fiction *When Christians Were Jews (That Is, Now),* subtitled *Recovering the Lost Jewishness of Christianity with the Gospel of Mark,* was published in 2006 by Cowley Publications. A novel, *The Retreatants,* was published in 2012 (Smashwords). A chapbook, *Christine Day, Love Poems,* was published in 2016 (Kittatuck Press). His novella, *Everything We Want,* was published in 2018 by Bloodstone Press. A poetry collection, *The Realm of Blessing,* was published in 2020 by Unsolicited Press. Alien Buddha Press has published his mystery novel *Noa(h) and the Bark* (2020), his novellas *The Request* and *Fall of the Medes*, (2021), and a short-story collection *The Lives and Spiritual Time of C.I. Abramovich* (2021). Wayne-Daniel lives in Mansfield, MA with his wife, the Lovely Christine.

www.ingramcontent.com/pod-product-compliance
Lightning Source LLC
Chambersburg PA
CBHW031149090426
42738CB00008B/1277